Coconut's
Words
Around the World

How do you say "friend" in Spanish?
"Dog" in Italian? "Cat" in German?

Travel around the world with Coconut
and Licorice and learn useful words and
phrases in eight languages!

In the first section, words are translated like this one:

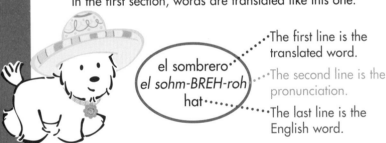

el sombrero····· ·····The first line is the
el sohm-BREH-roh····· translated word.
hat····· ·····The second line is the
 pronunciation.
·····The last line is the
 English word.

Syllables that appear in all capital letters, like *BREH* or *KAHT*,
show where the emphasis should be when the word is spoken.

My Name Is . . .

Me llamo Licorice.
meh YAH-moh Licorice
Spanish

Ich heiße Coconut.
eehk HIGH-seh Coconut
German

Wo jiao Licorice.
waw chiao Licorice
Mandarin Chinese

Je m'appelle Licorice.
zhuh mah-pell Licorice
French

Mi chiamo Coconut.
mee kee-AH-moh Coconut
Italian

Coconut to iimasu.
Coconut toh ee-mah-soo
Japanese

Friend

l'amica
lah-MEE-kah
Italian

l'amie
lah-mee
French

die Freundin
dee FROYN-din
German

mate
mite
Australian

hoaloha
hoh-ah-LOH-ha
Hawaiian

la amiga
lah ah-MEE-gah
Spanish

pengyou
puhng-yo
Mandarin Chinese

tomodachi
toh-moh-dah-chee
Japanese

France

Mexico

Germany

Japan

kumo
koo-moh
cloud
chō chō
choh choh
butterfly
asobiba
ah-so-bee-bah
playground
ranko
ahn-koh
ving
kōen
koh-en
park
suberidai
soo-beh-ree-dah-ee
slide
kirigirisu
kee-ree-jee-ree-soo
grasshopper
benchi
ben-chee
bench
kusa mura
koo-sah moo-rah
bush

China

kumu la'au
KOO-moo lah-ow
palm tree
niu
NEE-oo
coconut
pua
POO-ah
flower
'ukulele
oo-koo-LEH-leh
ukulele
pahukula
pah-hoo-KOO-lah
cooler
noho kahakai
NOH-hoh
kah-hah-KAH-ee
beach chair
hala kahiki
HAH-lah kah-HEE-kee
pineapple

Hawaii

Australia

Sit. Stay. Speak!

Good Morning

Guten Morgen
GOO-ten MOR-gen
German

Ohayo
oh-hah-yo
Japanese

Buenos días
BWEH-nohs DEE-ahs
Spanish

Bonjour
boh-zhoor
French

Buon giorno
bwohn JOR-noh
Italian

Zaoshang hao
dzaow-shung how
Mandarin Chinese

Aloha kakahiaka
ah-LOH-hah kah-kah-hee-AH-kah
Hawaiian

In the second section, words are translated like this one:

die Katze
dee KAHT-seh
German

·· ·The first line is the translated word.

·· ·The second line is the pronunciation.

·· ·The last line is the language.

First, learn several words from eight locations. Then turn to the back of the book for common English phrases with multiple translations. After you've had a chance to practice, you can teach your amigas, too!

Buona fortuna!

Good Night

Bonsoir
boh-swahr
French

Gute Nacht
GOO-teh NAKHT
German

Buenas noches
BWEH-nahs NOH-ches
Spanish

Oyasumi nasai
oh-yay-soo-mee nah-sah-ee
Japanese

Wan an
wahn ahn
Mandarin Chinese

Buona notte
BWOH-nah NOHT-teh
Italian

Aloha ahiahi
ah-LOH-hah ah-hee-AH-hee
Hawaiian

Hello

G'day
g'DYE
Australian

Hallo
HAHL-loh
German

Aloha
ah-LOH-hah
Hawaiian

Hola
OH-lah
Spanish

Ciao
chow
Italian

Salut
sah-loo
French

Ni hao
nee how
Mandarin Chinese

Konnichiwa
kohn-nee-chee-wah
Japanese

Girl

das Mädchen
dahs MAYD-chen
German

la jeune fille
lah jun fee
French

kaikamahine
kah-ee-kah-mah-HEE-neh
Hawaiian

la niña
lah NEEN-yah
Spanish

sheila
SHAY-lah
Australian

nu haizi
nyu high-dzuh
Mandarin Chinese

la ragazza
lah rah-GAHT-zah
Italian

onnanoko
on-nah-noh-koh
Japanese

Cool!

¡Fantástico!
fahn-TAHS-tee-koh
Spanish

Fantastique !
fahn-tahs-teek
French

Zhen bang!
jun bahng
Mandarin Chinese

'Olu'olu!
OH-loo-OH-loo
Hawaiian

Klasse!
CLAS-seh
German

Bonzer!
BON-zer
Australian

Cute!

¡Linda!
LEEN-dah
Spanish

Kawaii!
kah-wah-ee
Japanese

Carina!
kah-REE-nah
Italian

Niedlich!
NEED-lick
German

Adorable !
ah-doh-rah-bleh
French

Nani!
nah-nee
Hawaiian

Ke ai!
kuh eye
Mandarin Chinese

Spiffy!
SPIF-ee
Australian

Dog

el perro
el PAIR-roh
Spanish

inu
ee-noo
Japanese

le chien
luh shee-en
French

il cane
eel KAH-neh
Italian

'ilio
ee-LEE-oh
Hawaiian

der Hund
dair hoont
German

gou
go
Mandarin Chinese

Cat

el gato
el GAH-toh
Spanish

neko
neh-koh
Japanese

le chat
luh shah
French

pōpoki
POH-poh-kee
Hawaiian

il gatto
eel GAHT-toh
Italian

die Katze
dee KAHT-seh
German

mao
maow
Mandarin Chinese

Please

Bitte
BIT-teh
German

S'il vous plaît
seel voo pleh
French

Por favor
por fah-VOR
Spanish

Per favore
pair fah-VOH-reh
Italian

Hō'olu
HOH-oh-loo
Hawaiian

Onegai
oh-neh-gah-ee
Japanese

Qing
ching
Mandarin Chinese

Thank You

Gracias
GRAH-see-ahs
Spanish

Merci
mair-see
French

Xiexie ni
shyeh-shyeh nee
Mandarin Chinese

Danke
DAHN-keh
German

Arigatō
ah-ree-gah-toh
Japanese

Grazie
GRAH-zee-eh
Italian

Mahalo
mah-HAH-loh
Hawaiian

Happy Birthday!

¡Feliz cumpleaños!
feh-LEEZ koom-pleh-AHN-yohs
Spanish

Bon anniversaire !
bohn ahn-nee-vair-sair
French

Hau'oli lā hānau!
HAH-oo-OH-lee LAH HAH-noh-oo
Hawaiian

Shengri kuai le!
sheng-reh kweye luh
Mandarin Chinese

Otanjōbi omedeto!
oh-tahn-joh-bee oh-meh-deh-toh
Japanese

Buon compleanno!
bwohn kohm-pleh-AHN-noh
Italian

Herzlichen Glückwünsch zum Geburtstag!
*HAIRTS-lee-khen GLOOK-voonsh
tsoom geh-BOORTS-tahk*
German

Yum!

Di gusto!
dee GOOS-toh
Italian

C'est bon !
say boh
French

Hao chi!
how chuhr
Mandarin Chinese

¡Delicioso!
deh-lee-see-OH-zoh
Spanish

Lecker!
LEK-er
German

Squisito!
skwee-ZEE-toh
Italian

Oishii!
oo-ee-she-ee
Japanese

'Ono loa!
OH-noh LOH-ah
Hawaiian

Good Luck!

Ganbatte!
gum-bat-teh
Japanese

Buona fortuna!
BWOH-nah for-TOO-nah
Italian

Pōmaika'i!
POH-mah-ee-KAH-ee
Hawaiian

Bonne chance !
bun shahns
French

Viel Glück!
feel glook
German

¡Buena suerte!
BWEH-nah soo-AIR-teh
Spanish

Zhuni hao yun!
joo-nee how yuhn
Mandarin Chinese

Good-bye

A hui hou
a HOO-e hoe
Hawaiian

Sayōnara
sah-yoh-nah-rah
Japanese

Arrivederci
ah-ree-veh-DAIR-chee
Italian

Hooroo
Australian

Adiós
ah-dee-OHS
Spanish

Au revoir
oh reh-vwahr
French

Zai jian
dzye yan
Mandarin Chinese

Auf Wiedersehen
owf VEE-der-zay-en
German

I Love You

Je t'aime
zheh tem
French

Ti amo
tee AH-moh
Italian

Ich liebe dich
eekh LEE-beh deekh
German

Te amo
teh AH-moh
Spanish

Wo ai ni
wah eye nee
Mandarin Chinese

Ai shiteru
Eye she-tuh-roo
Japanese

She cooks! She cracks secret
codes! She tells jokes!
What type of Coconut book
would you like to read next?

Send your ideas to:
Coconut Book Editor
American Girl
8400 Fairway Place
Middleton, WI 53562

Here are some other
Coconut books you might like:

❏ I read it.

❏ I read it.

❏ I read it.

❏ I read it.

❏ I read it.

❏ I read it.